My Sketchbook:

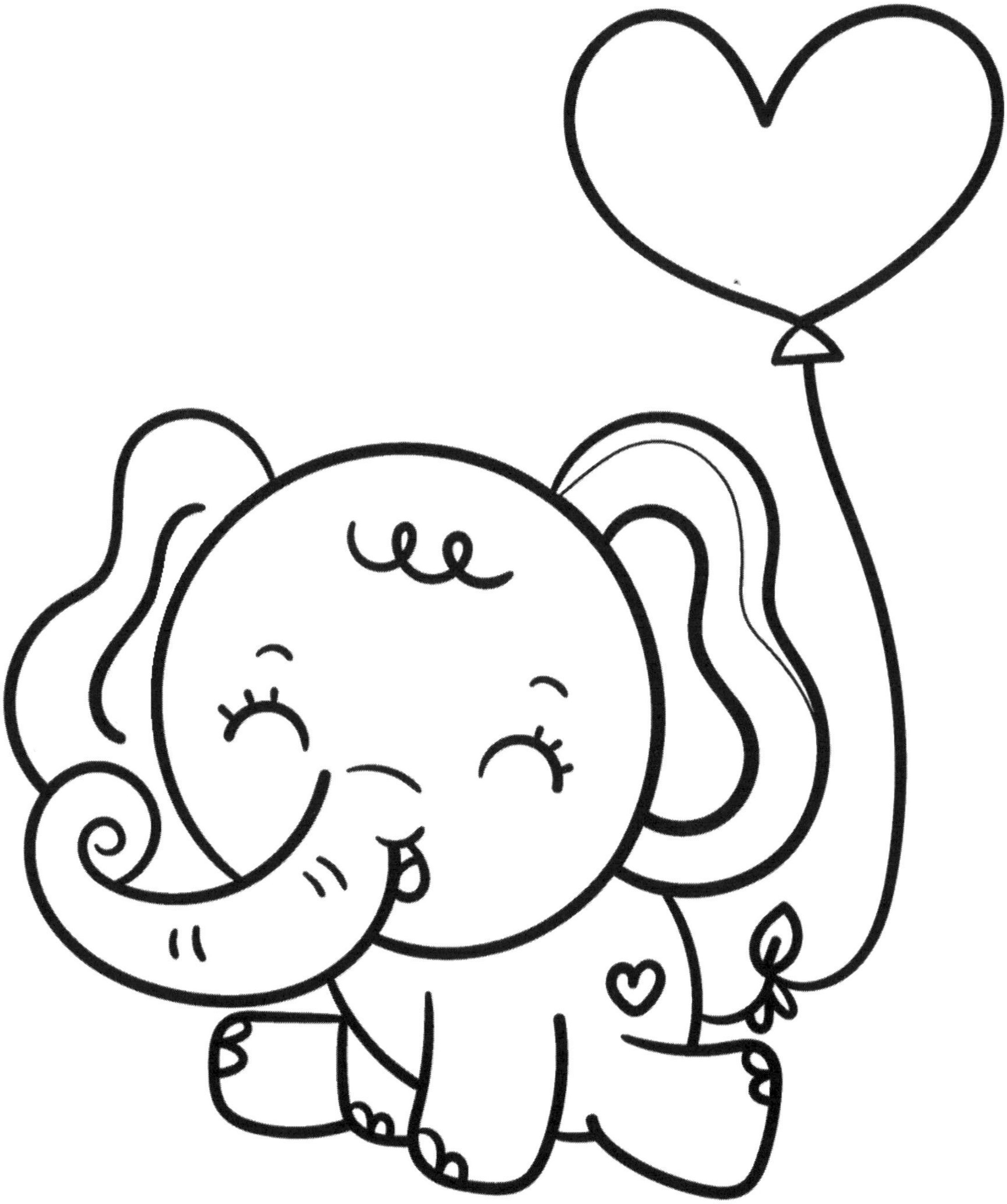

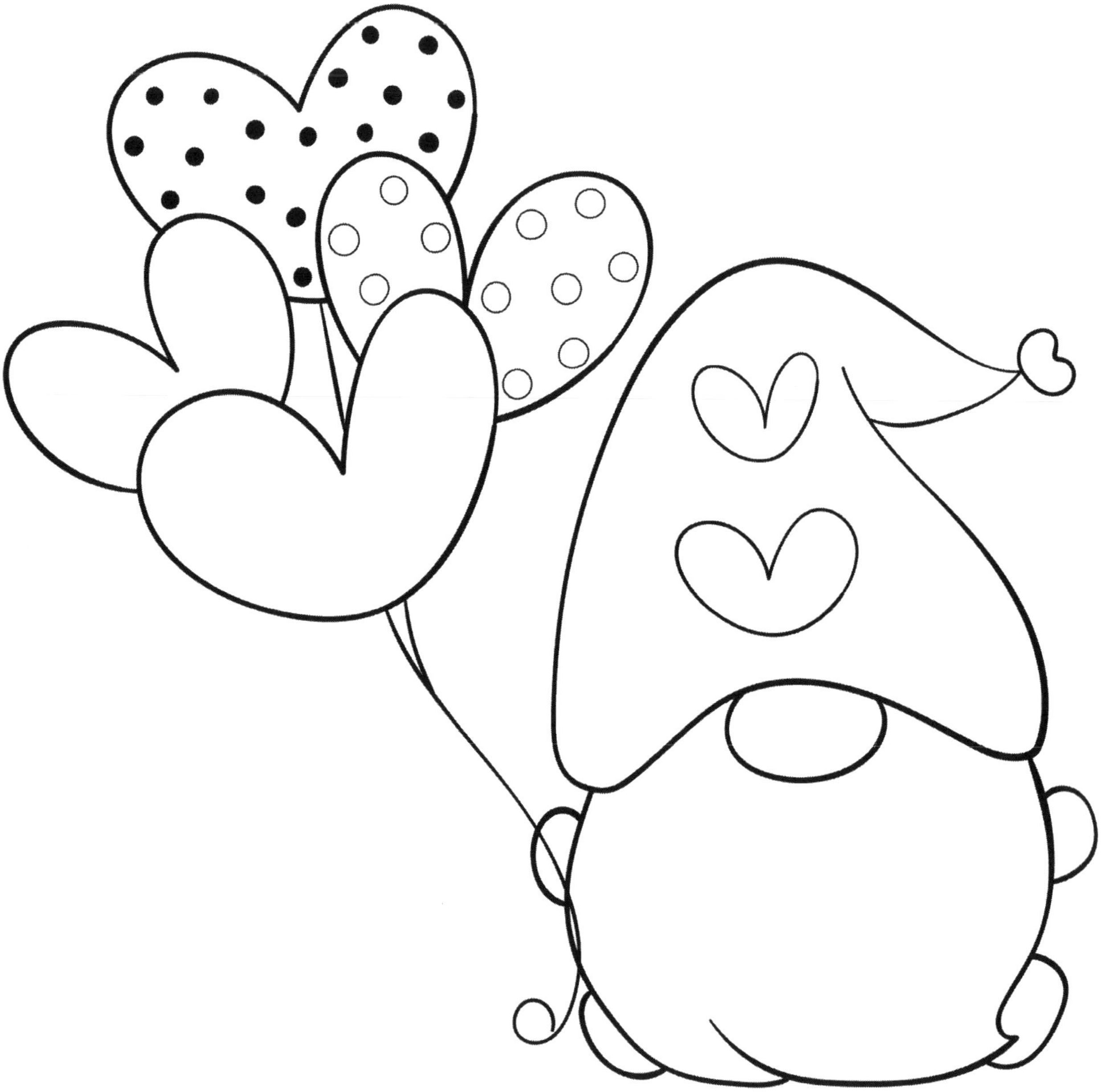

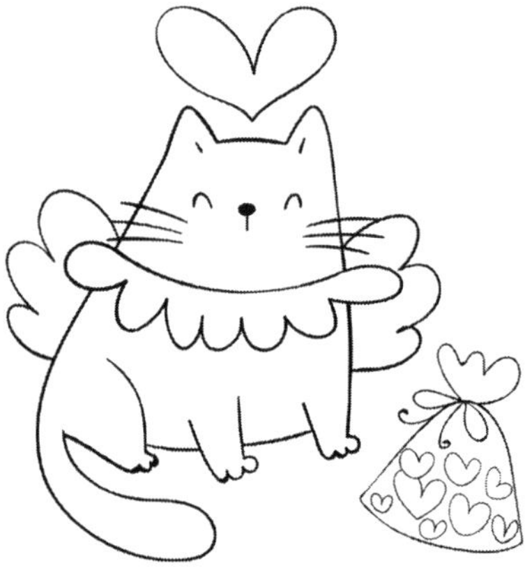

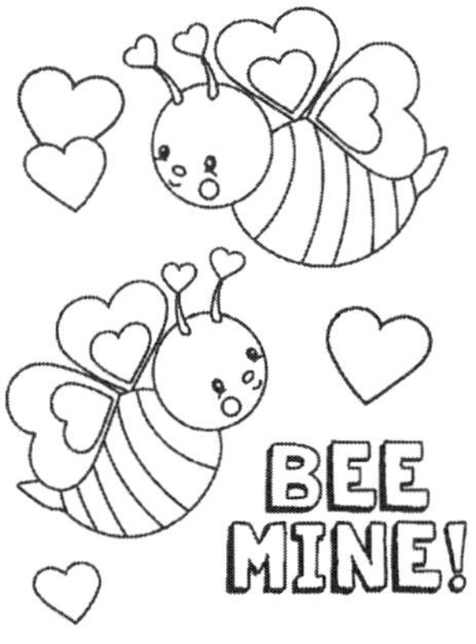
BEE
MINE!

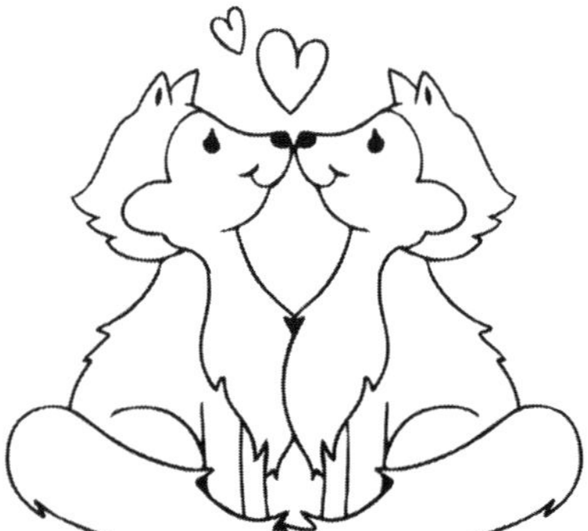

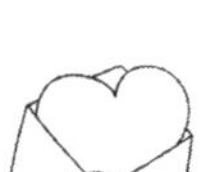

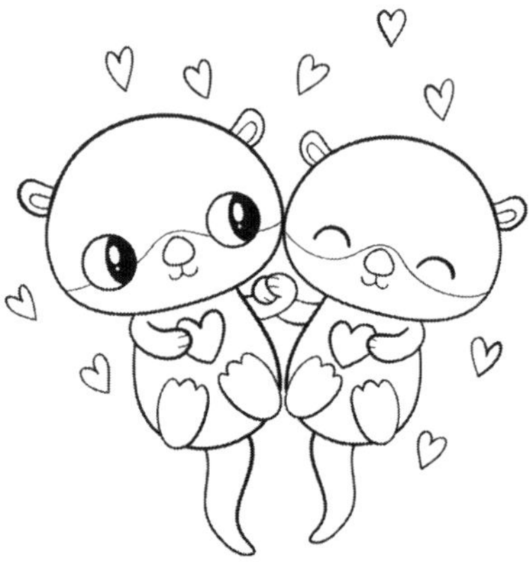

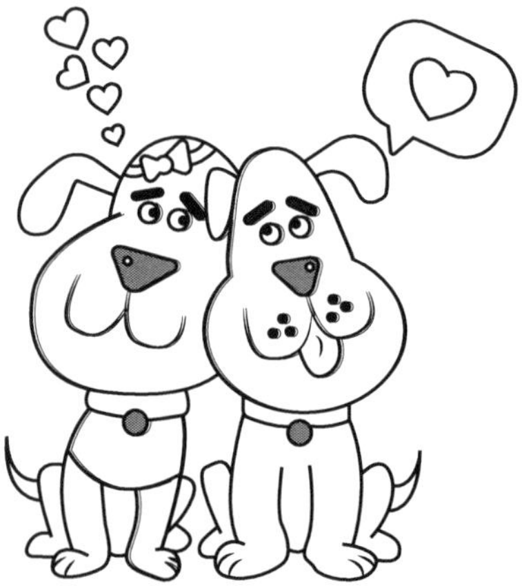

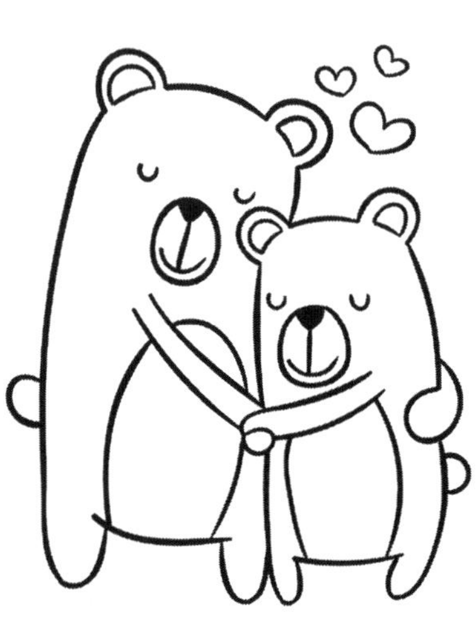

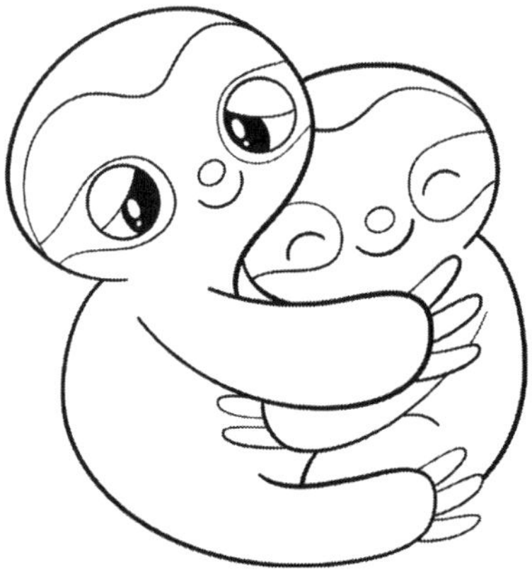

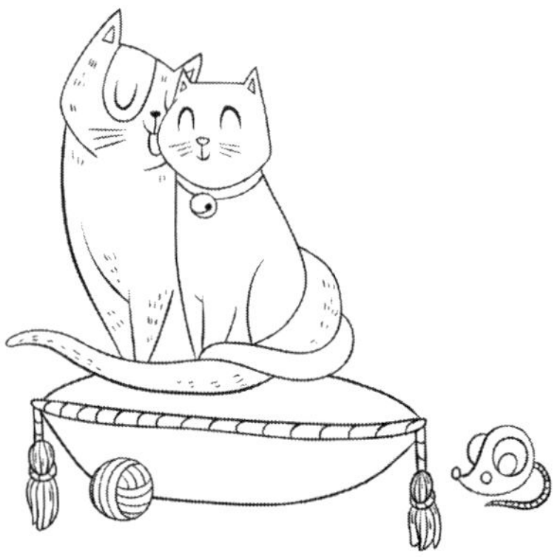

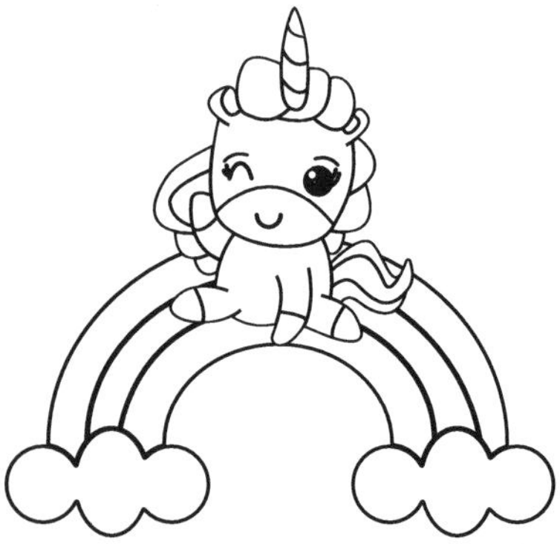

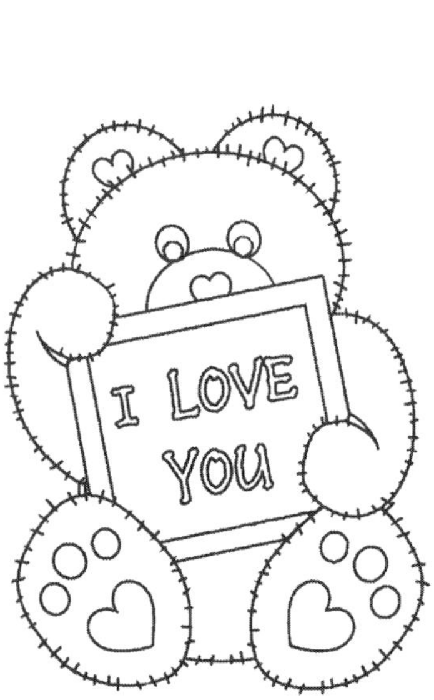
I LOVE YOU

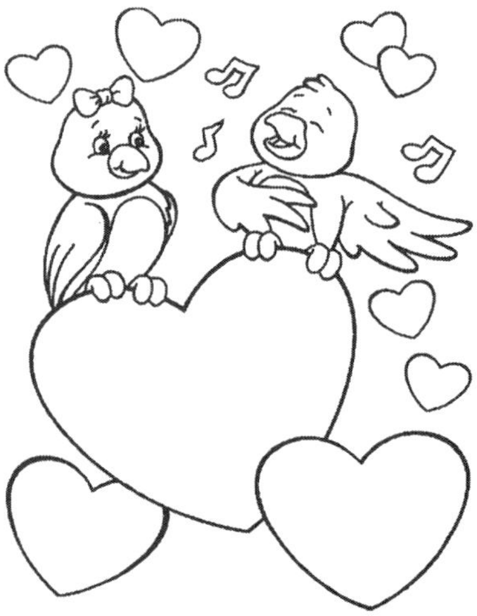

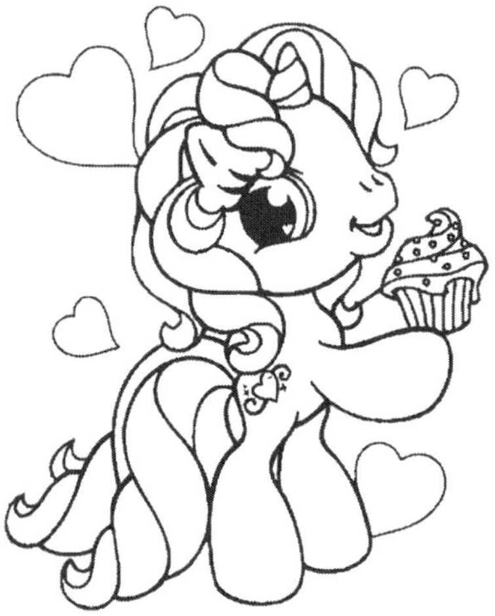

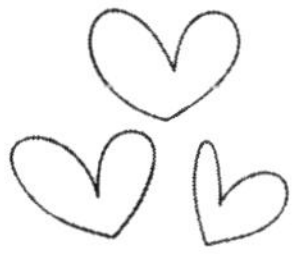

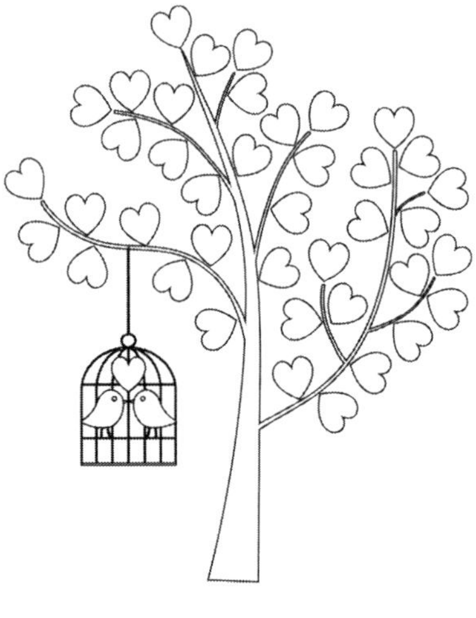

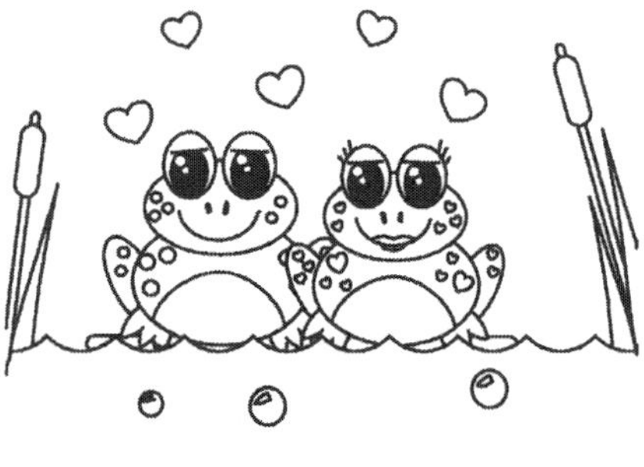

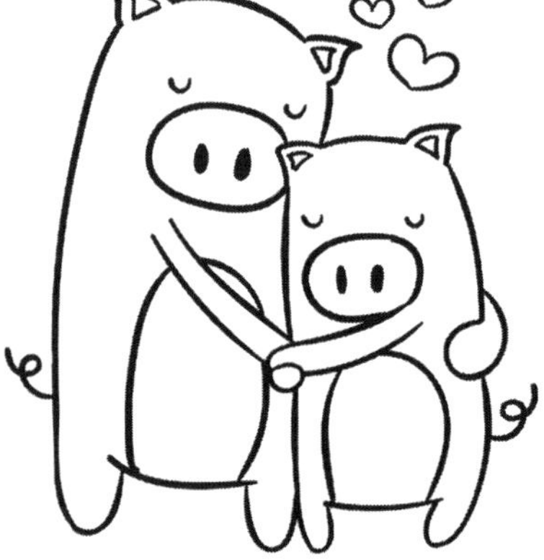

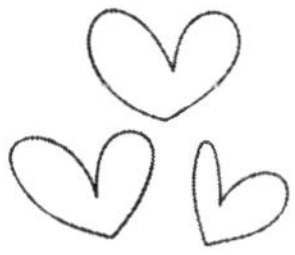

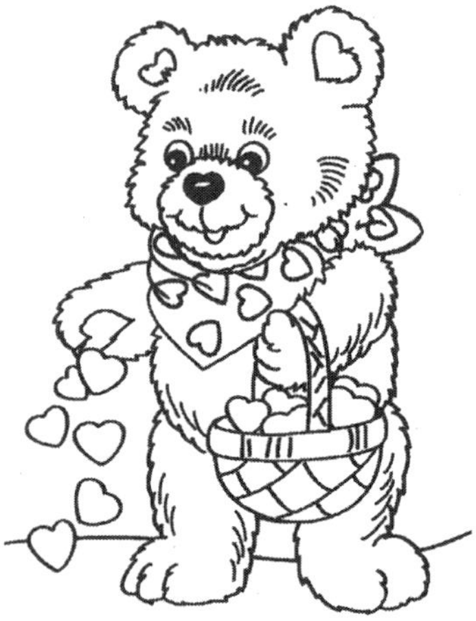

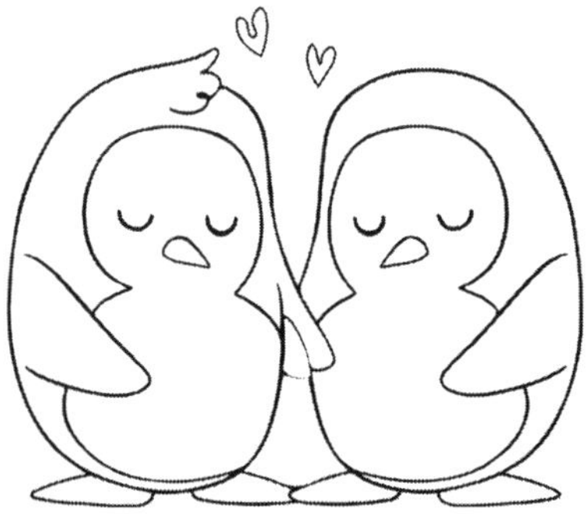

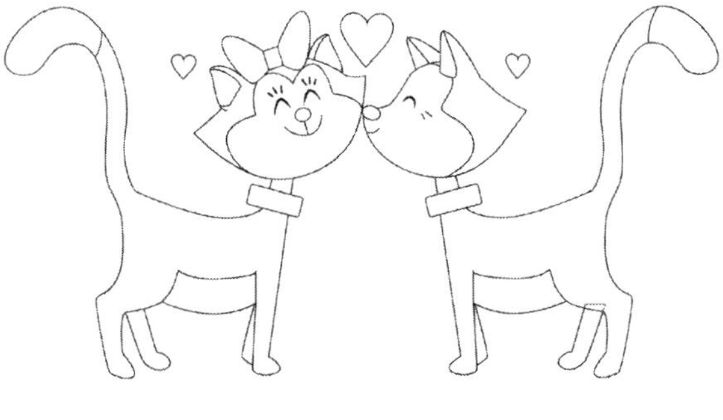

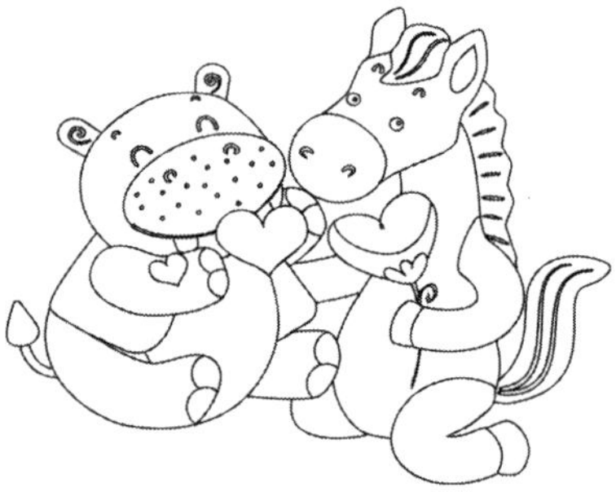

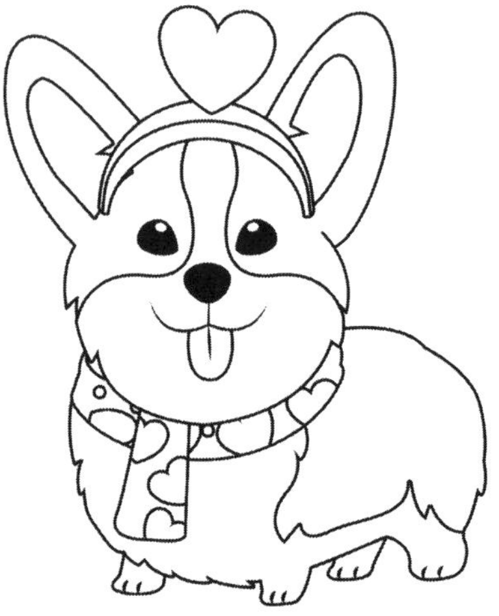

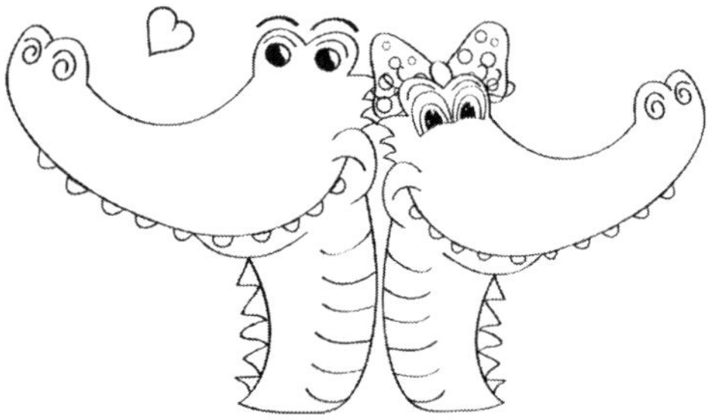

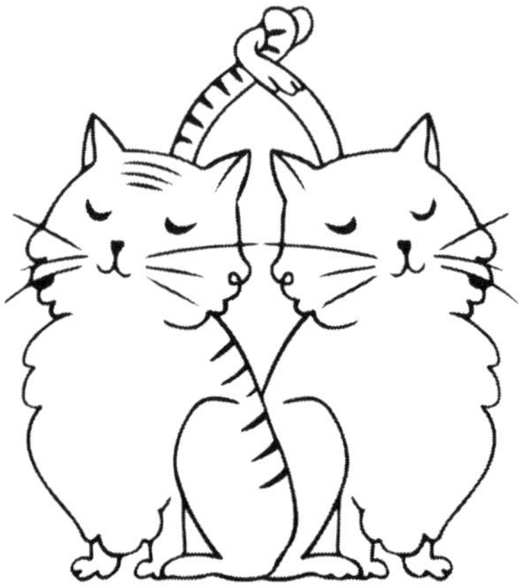

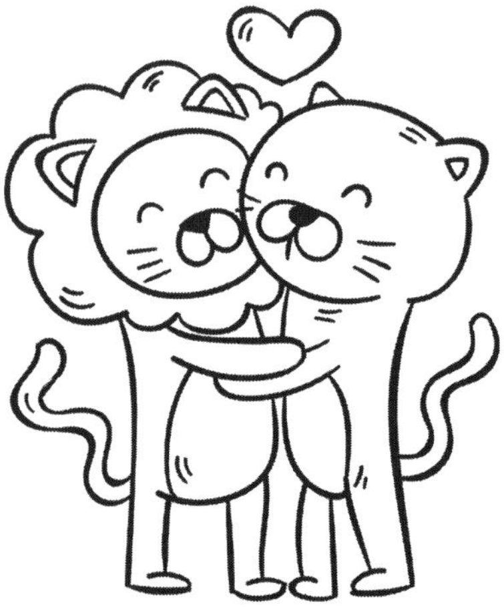

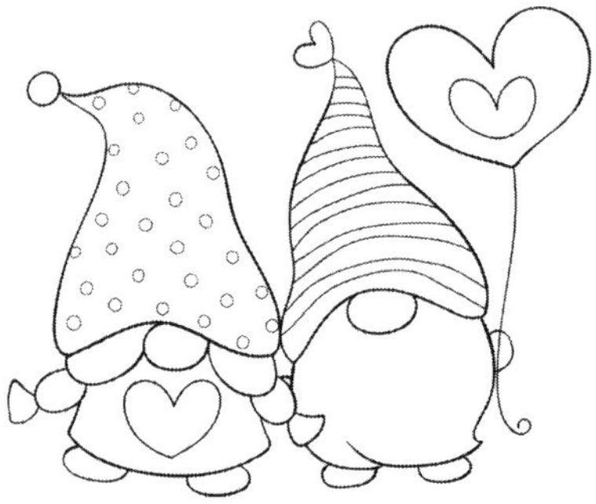

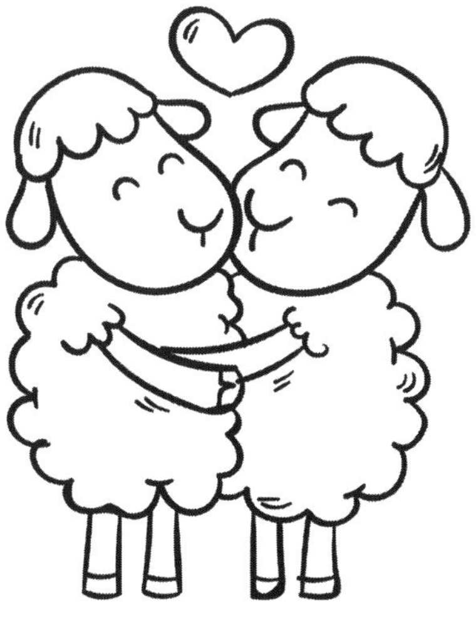

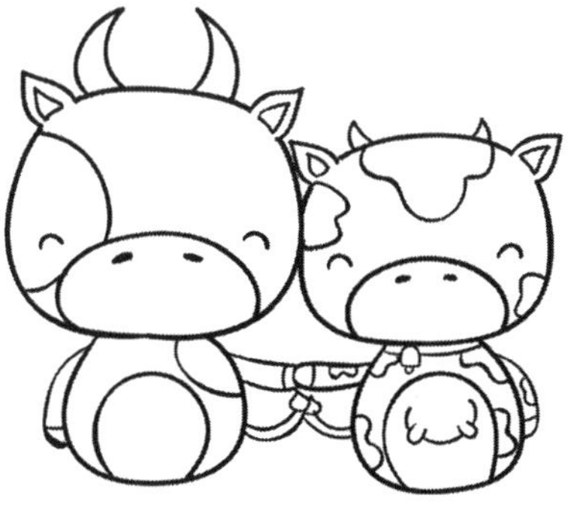

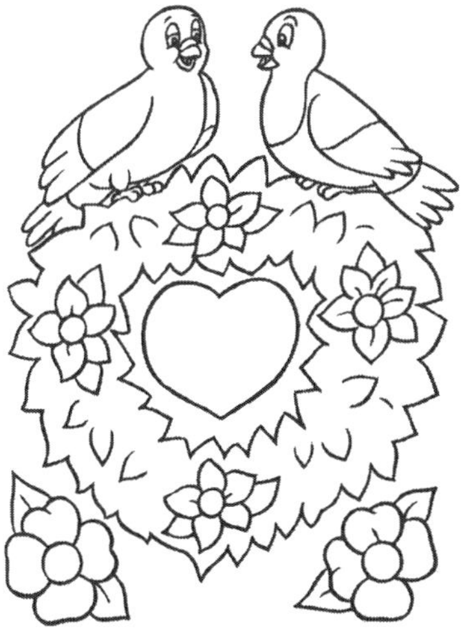

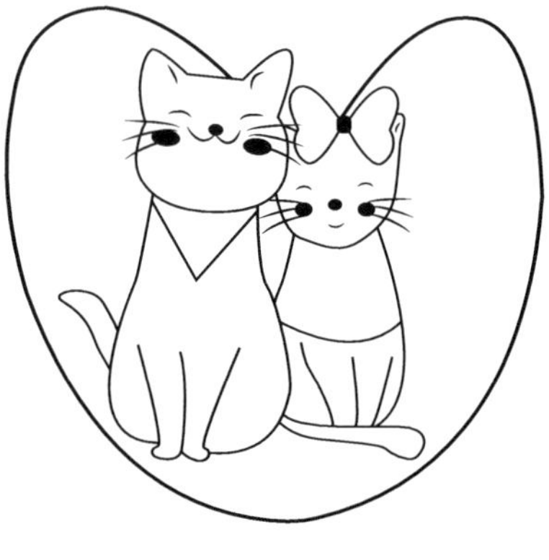

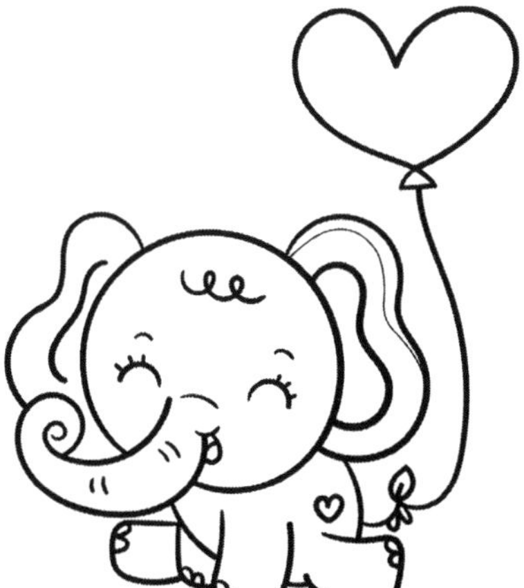

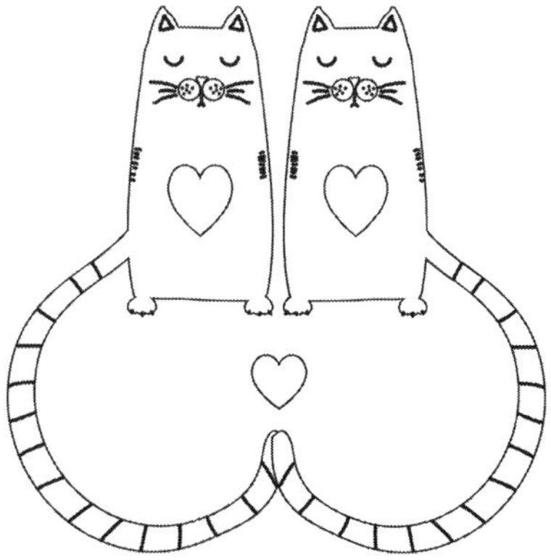

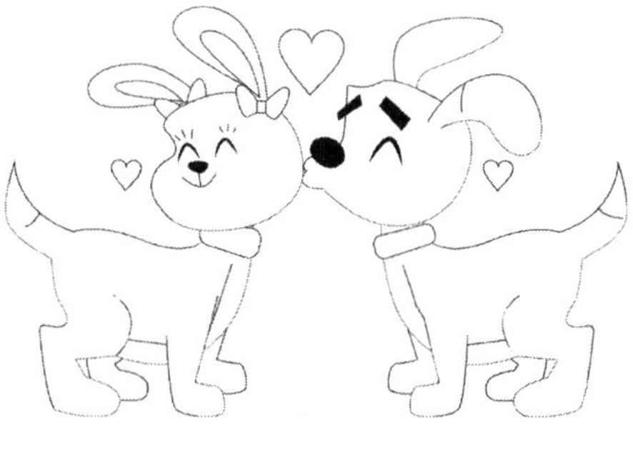

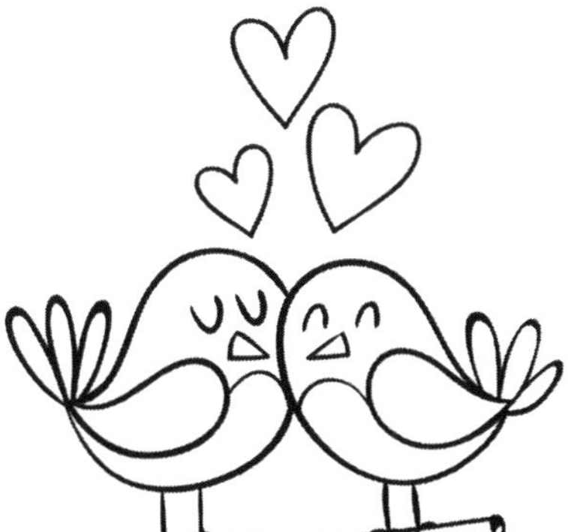

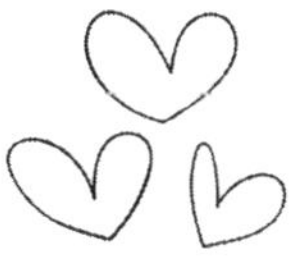

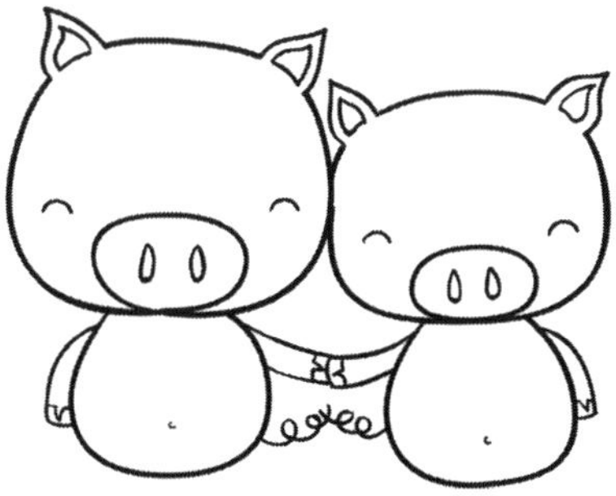

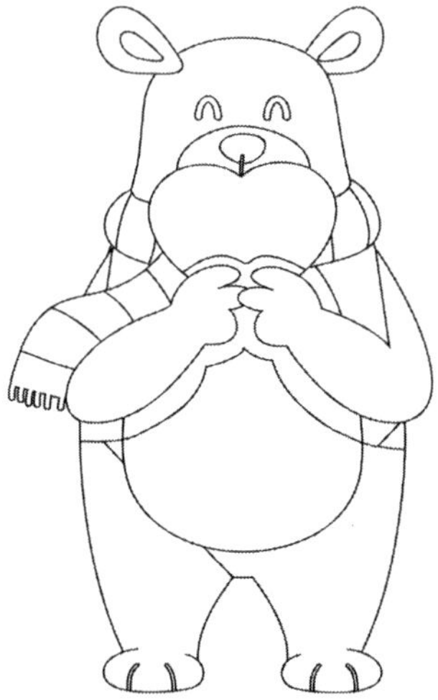

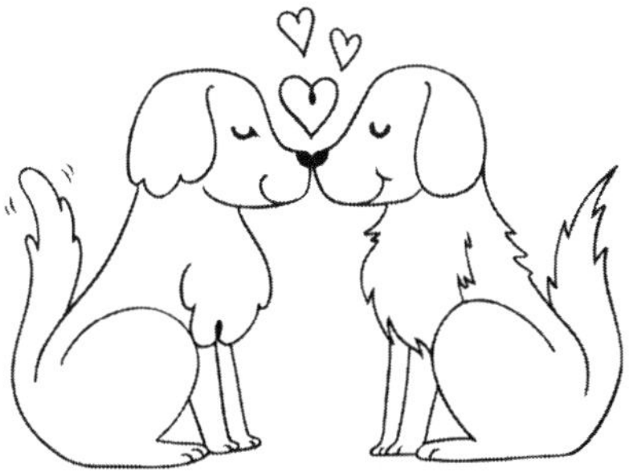

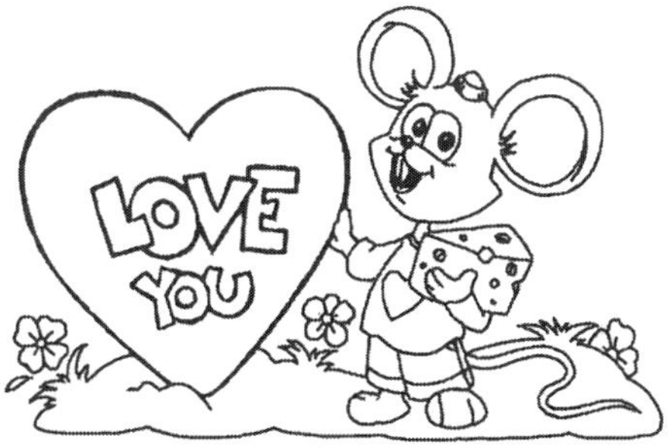
LOVE
YOU

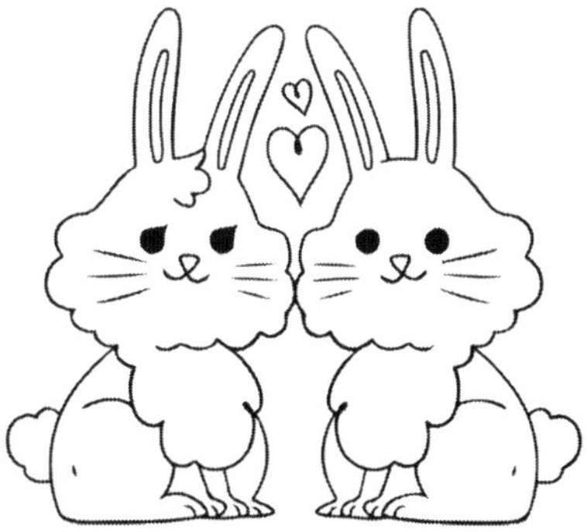

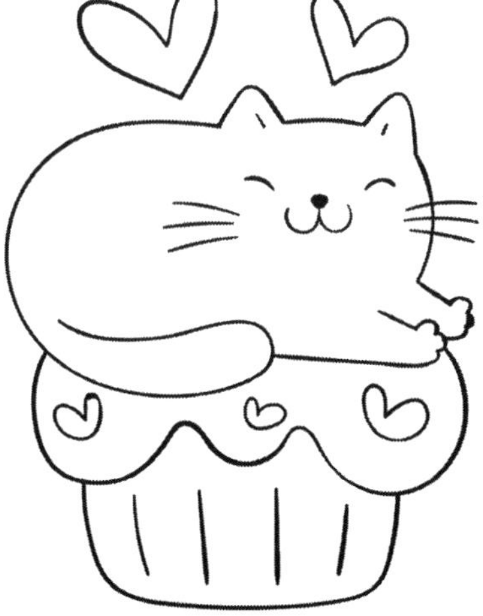

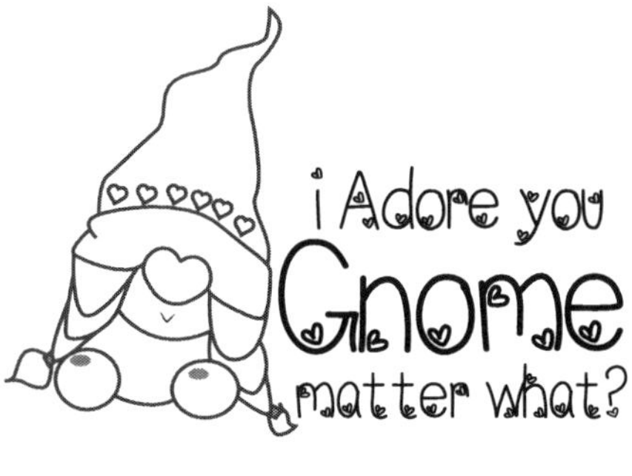
i Adore you
Gnome
matter what?

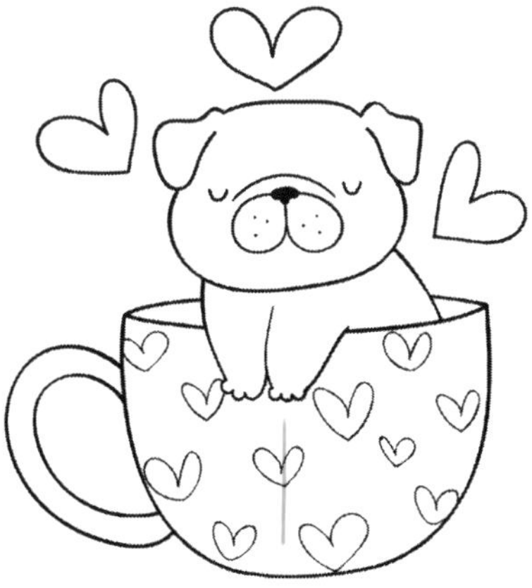

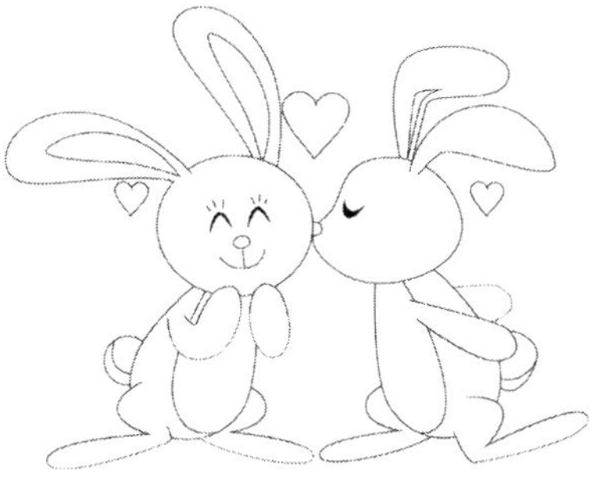

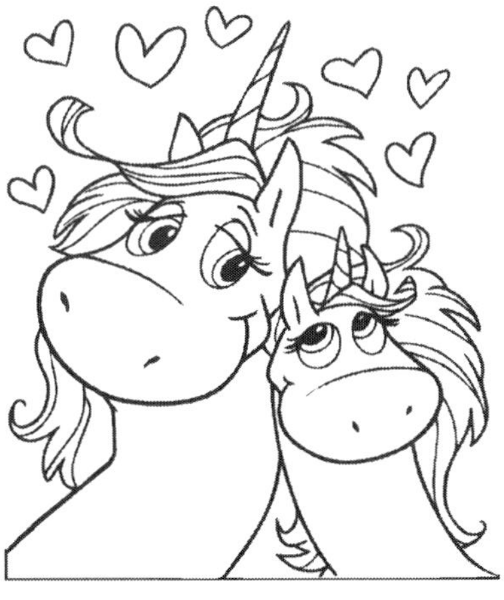

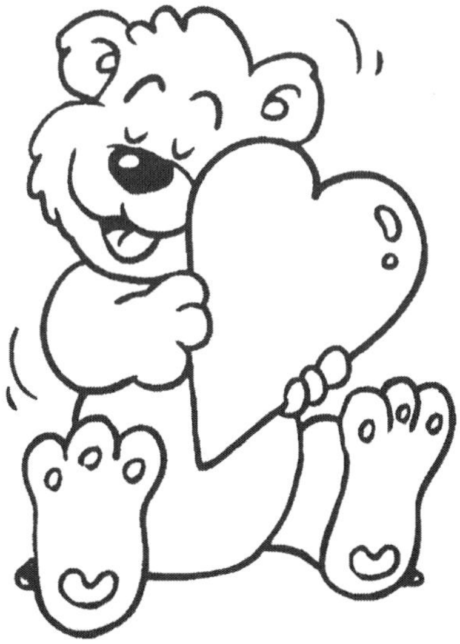

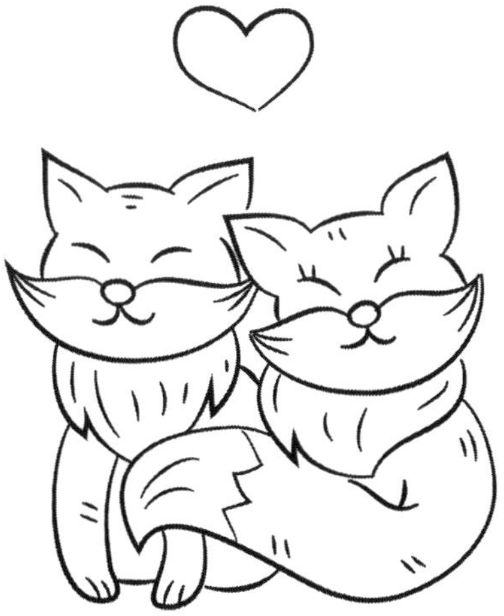

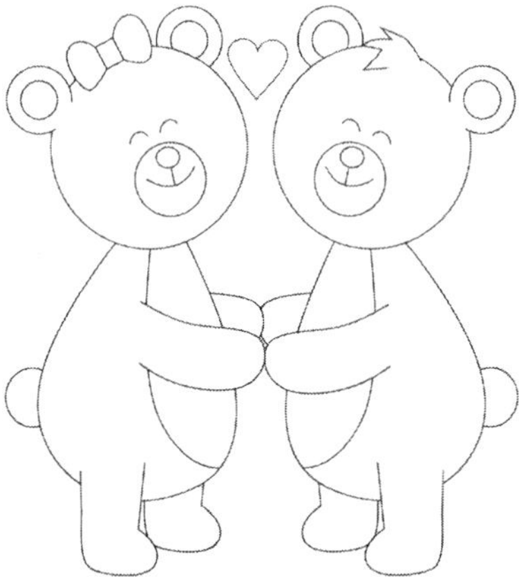

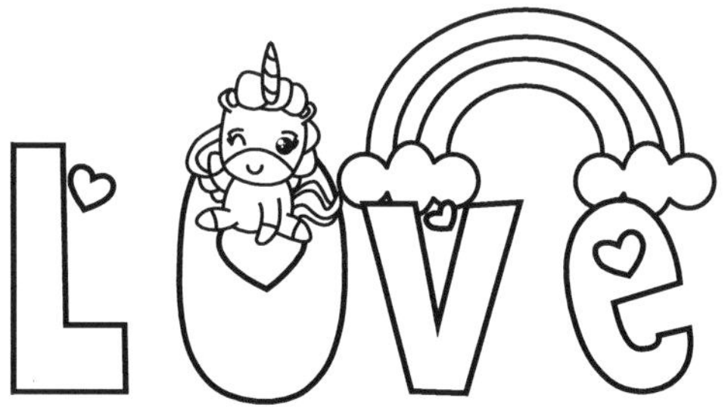
LOVE

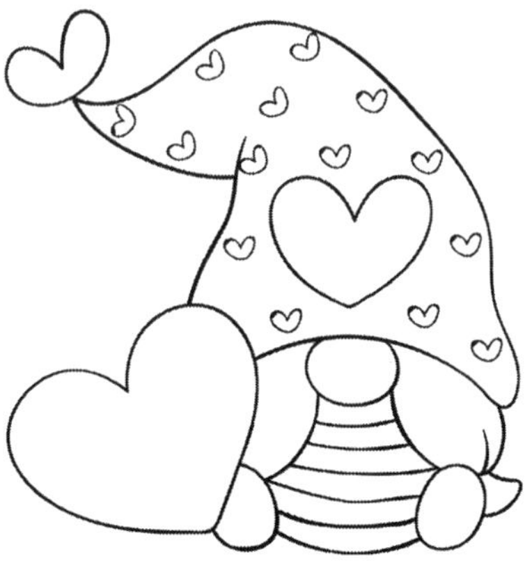

Super Adorable Valentines Theme

Sketchbook For Kids

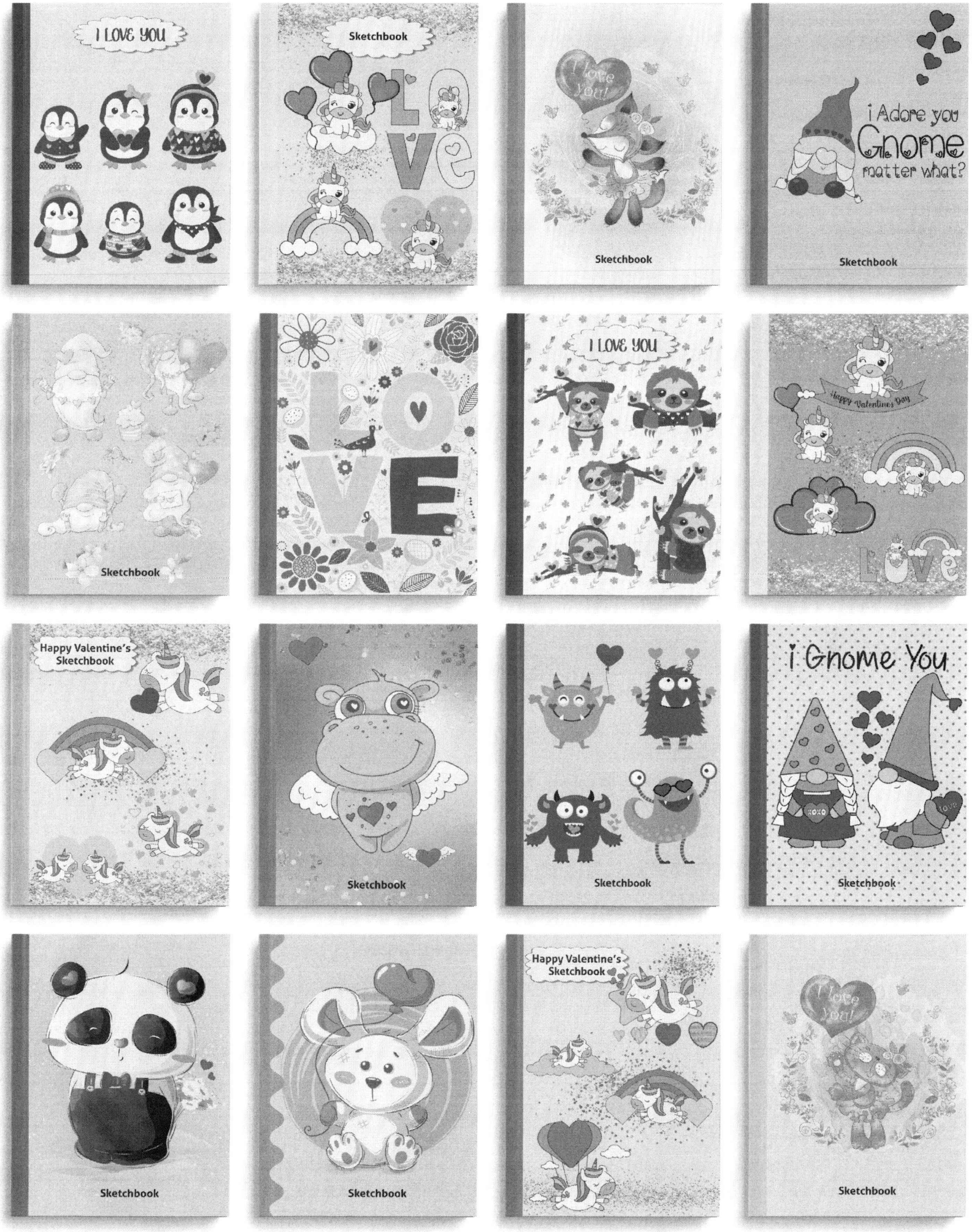

Made in the USA
Monee, IL
08 February 2022

90877385R00059